CORNISH BAGPIPES,
Fact or Fiction?

By
Harry Woodhouse

DYLLANSOW TRURAN

**First published in 1994
by Dyllansow Truran
Trewolsta, Trewirgie, Kernow (Cornwall)**

Copyright © 1994 Harry Woodhouse

ISBN 1 85022 070 0

Printed in Great Britain
Typeset, Printed and Bound by Troutbeck Press,
a subsidiary of R. Booth (Bookbinder) Limited
Antron Hill, Mabe, Penryn, Cornwall

"THE MERRY BAGPIPES", 16TH-17TH CENTURY WOODCUT
"Bagpipes in English Works of Art" by Dr R. D. Cannon,
Galpin Society Journal, Volume XLII

Contents

Foreword

Mystery surrounds the whole idea of Cornish bagpipes: was there ever such an instrument; could it be revived; where were they played, and what for? In the following pages Harry Woodhouse takes us through the history and known facts about this instrument, the relationship with other similar instruments, and the current revival of interest. But be warned, behind Harry's relaxed style of writing and delightful anecdotes is a very sharp scientific mind bearing on the subject.

PYBUGH MENSTREL COLONNEK, MAY HYLLYN DONSIA DYSON!

Merv Davey,
Pybyor Gorseth Kernow.
(honorary piper to the Cornish Gorsedd.)

THE AUTHOR WITH HIS HOME-MADE CORNISH BAGPIPES

Photo: Raymond Hitchcock

About the Author

Harry Woodhouse was born in St. Austell in 1930 and went from St. Austell Grammar School to Queens' College Cambridge where he obtained his M.A. in Natural Sciences. He spent most of his working life as a manager for English China Clays, and his last job was to set up their Pacific office in Singapore where he lived with his wife until his retirement back to Cornwall.

An enthusiastic musical amateur, he has played the clarinet with the Cornwall Symphony Orchestra and other Cornish orchestras for over twenty years, and with a group of musical friends, he gives lectures/recitals for charity about the "Old Church Gallery Minstrels" who played in our churches and chapels before they had organs. He is a member of the Galpin Society, and studies ancient musical instruments, making copies of them in his workshop. He plays the serpent and the ophicleide and has made several TV appearances, including a short sequence in the "Poldark" series. He is a Bard of the Cornish Gorsedd.

Harry writes occasional articles for magazines, but this is his first effort at writing a book. He says he enjoyed writing it immensely. We hope you enjoy reading it just as much.

Chapter 1

BEHOLD! I TELL YOU A MYSTERY

Mention the word "bagpipes" today and we all think of Scotland. Indeed Scottish bagpipes are played today all over the world, and excellent models are manufactured in India and Pakistan. However, Welsh and Irish history books also contain references to their bagpipes, and a visit to a museum with a good collection of musical instruments, such as the Horniman museum in Dulwich, or the Pitt Rivers Museum in Oxford reveals weird and wonderful bagpipes from all over the world.

The bagpipe is indeed a very ancient instrument, with a history going back over a thousand years. It has a good recorded history in Scotland, Ireland, Wales and Brittany. Why do we never hear about the Cornish bagpipes? Was there ever such a thing?

This little book is not a scholarly textbook, but a layman's guide to the answers to these fascinating questions. If you are still awake and interested when you get to the end there are many scholarly books to lead you further up this intriguing path.

Chapter 2

WHAT IS A BAGPIPE?

A bagpipe is a highly specialised example of a woodwind instrument. There are three ways of making a more or less musical sound with your mouth and a hollow tube. You can blow across a hole in the end as if playing the panpipes. The flute family of instruments work like this. You can purse your lips together and press them against the tube, while forcing air between them to produce a sort of "raspberry". The trumpet family of instruments work like this. You can insert two pieces of flat cane fastened close together with a narrow slit between, put them between your lips and blow. The reed family of instruments work like this, including the oboe, bassoon, and bagpipes. When I was at college I bought a bassoon in a junk shop for £5. The owner thought it was an oboe. I practised for months, then proudly sat down and played a tune to my rather non-musical father. When I had finished, he said "I can make a better noise than that without an instrument".

The hollow tube not only supports the lips or canes, but its length encourages the vibrations to sound a musical note, rather than just a noise. The column of air inside the tube resonates at a frequency dependent mainly on its length - the longer the tube, the lower the note. Many different ways have been worked out for playing different notes. The obvious way is to have a tube for each note, and this is done in the panpipes. One note at a time can be played by moving a different pipe under the lips. The pipe organ uses the same principle, but this can play several notes at once by using a complicated system of levers attached to a keyboard. Another way is to have a sliding tube so that the length can be varied continuously. This is not very practical with wood, but the trombone uses sliding brass tubes, and this works very well. The trombone is the only orchestral wind instrument which can slide up and down the musical scale like a violin, not being bound by notes fixed by the maker. The most common way of getting different notes is to bore a row of holes down the length of the hollow tube, and cover them with your fingers one at a time. The more fingers put down, the longer the tube, and thus the lower the note. Of course, the maker has to fix the diameter of the holes, and the distance between them, to give some sort of musical scale. All woodwind instruments except the panpipes use this principle - the oboe, clarinet, flute, saxophone, bassoon, and the bagpipes. Wide instruments like the saxophone, and long instruments like the bassoon have to use metal keys to cover the holes, because the fingers are not wide enough or long enough to cope. Also the Lord has only blessed us with 8 fingers and 2 thumbs, so to play more notes than this, metal keys are fitted to all modern orchestral woodwind instruments. The keys not only impress your friends, but actually make the instrument easier to play.

Although flutes, clarinets and oboes are all called woodwind instruments, they can be made of other materials without affecting the sound too much. Modern flutes are nearly all made of metal, and old ones were occasionally made of ivory. Cheap clarinets and oboes are nowadays often made of plastic. Metal clarinets are very popular in the USA where they are used by marching bands who cannot rush indoors when it starts to rain. They also survive better when children drop them, or sit on them.

So much for the tube, or resonator. The actual sound generator of a wind instrument is called the reed, even if it is not actually made of reed. Trumpets are "lip-reed" instruments - it is the lips themselves which vibrate and produce the sound. Woodwind instruments which use actual reeds are divided into two classes. Oboes and bassoons use a double reed, and clarinets and saxophones use a single reed. Bagpipes use both types.

Double reeds were probably the first type to be invented, and were made by tying together two bits of flat grass or reed with a narrow slot between. They were later made more reliable by starting with a cylindrical piece of cane or rush and splitting it in half lengthways. The two ends were then folded back on themselves and tied with string. The fold was then cut open, and scraped with a knife until it was very thin. To make the thing strong the other end was tied with string to a tiny tube of metal called a staple. Double reeds for oboes, bassoons and bagpipes are all made like this today. Really keen musicians make their own, but most just buy them from the local music shop.

The single reed system is a bit more complicated. Clarinet and saxophone reeds are just flat pieces of cane scraped very thin at one end. However, to make them sound, they are pressed on to the flat part of a mouthpiece called a table. This table is not perfectly flat, but falls away under the tip of the reed to enable the air to get under it and let it vibrate.

Bagpipe single reeds are made from a piece of cylindrical cane with a knot at one end to close it off. A blade or tongue is formed in the side by cutting a slit with a sharp knife. It can be cut upwards towards the closed end, or downwards towards the open end. The open end is inserted into the pipe. To make the tongue vibrate at all, some air must be able to get underneath it, so it is either prised slightly up, or a hair is inserted under the base.

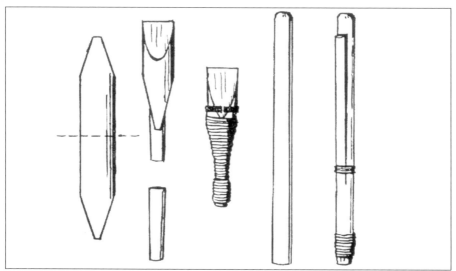

BAGPIPE REED MAKING: CHANTER (LEFT) AND DRONE (RIGHT)
"Woodwind Instruments & Their History" by Anthony Baines. Faber & Faber

If you think all this is getting a bit complicated, I have to tell you that there is yet another way to classify woodwind instruments, and that is by the shape of their bore. Clarinets have cylindrical bores, that is, the diameter of the bore is the same all the way through. They produce the soft liquid tone we all recognise from Acker Bilk or Mozart's clarinet concerto. The sound only contains odd multiples of the principal frequency being sounded, and if the reed is squeezed harder, and a tiny hole opened near the top of the tube, the note jumps up one and a half octaves, that is, to three times the frequency. Clarinets have a bell on the bottom, but this is only to improve the tone of the bottom notes, and does not change the basic principles of the cylindrical bore. As we have seen, the clarinet always uses a single reed, but a double reed can also be used with a cylindrical bore, and this is done in the bagpipe practice chanter, to produce a soft sweet sound

14

for practising indoors.

Oboes, bassoons and most bagpipe chanters have conical bores, that is, the diameter increases from the reed end to the bell end. The quality of the sound depends, amongst other things, on the profile of the cone.

Shawms (ancestors of the oboe) have short wide cones, like ice-cream cornets, and make ear-splitting noises suitable for the town waits to get everybody out of bed in the morning. Oboes make a gentler sound, and bassoons, with their very long slow taper, a sound even more muted and muffled. "Overblowing" a conical tube causes the note to rise by exactly one octave, but this is not normally possible on the bagpipes, since the reed is not between the player's lips but inaccessible inside the bagpipe stock. Saxophones are unusual in combining a conical bore with a single reed like that of a clarinet. They produce a sensuous juicy sound.

Oboes, clarinets, flutes, saxophones and bassoons can only play one note at a time. However, in ancient times two pipes were often played at once. They were either tied together in parallel, or splayed slightly apart as divergent pipes. The fingers could be shared between the two pipes to play a somewhat limited scale on each pipe. Since most musicians are human, they have to breathe from time to time, and this can be a nuisance when playing long folk melodies. In ancient times the only way this problem could be solved was by the player puffing out his cheeks to form a small bag, then snatching a quick breath through his nose whilst supplying the air from the mouth. It is said that the goddess Athene gave up playing the pipes when she discovered that it gave her bloodshot eyes and swollen cheeks. The effect became called "the disfigurement of Athene". Players on the shawn in Africa and elsewhere still puff out their cheeks like this when playing. Many years ago I heard a group of them playing for the belly-dancers in Bou Saada in Algeria. They turned their backs on the naked ladies so as not to offend Allah. I thought they got their bloodshot eyes by trying to peer backwards.

As a sort of half-way stage to the bagpipes, the bladder-pipe was invented, with an animal bladder like a balloon between the mouth and the pipe. Then somebody, somewhere, hit on the idea of using a bag which could be placed under the arm, and squeezed to give a constant air supply while the player was taking a breath.

Now at last we can say what bagpipes are. They consist of a bag, usually fed with air by a mouthpipe or blowpipe, and fitted with one or more pipes sounded by single or double reeds. One or two of the pipes can be bored

BLADDER-PIPE, 14TH CENTURY WALL PAINTING
"Musical Instruments through the Ages" by Dr Buchner. Spring Books,

with fingerholes, when they are called chanters, or may simply sound one note, when they are called drones. The Scottish Highland Bagpipe, by far the best known, has a single conical chanter fitted with a double reed, and three cylindrical drones fitted with single reeds.

Originally the bag was made of the whole skin of a sheep or goat, which might have been pickled in brine or alum, or treated with fat or just left in its natural state. In some cases the wool was left on, either on the outside or else the whole thing was turned inside out. It must have soon become extremely smelly, and I don't think I would want to sit next to the bagpiper or borrow his instrument.

The chanter was usually fitted to the neck of the defunct animal, and the blowpipe and a drone fitted to the forelegs. The back end was usually sewn up, but perhaps sometimes the blowpipe was attached at the rear end, giving rise to some rather vulgar prose from Aristophanes.

A SPLENDID EXAMPLE OF A DOUBLE CHANTER BAGPIPE WITH THE FUR
LEFT ON THE OUTSIDE. THIS ONE IS A ZUKRA FROM SAUDI ARABIA
"Folk Music Instruments of the World" by A. Buchner. Octopus Books

17

Instead of using the whole animal skin, the bladder or stomach of a larger animal such as cow was sometimes used. Psychologically, this seems even more revolting.

Such animal bags are still used in primitive bagpipes, but nowadays in western society tanned leather is used, cut out from a pattern and sewn. Mackintosh and rubber bags are occasionally used, but although this seems a good idea in theory, in practice the bags collect water and the reeds soon get water-logged. Leather has the property of absorbing considerable amounts of water, while still being reasonably airtight. To make the bag completely airtight, all sorts of concoctions are poured inside to seal the leather and the stitching. I have heard of black treacle, lard, gelatine, molasses, tallow and porridge (similar materials are recommended for putting in your car radiator when it leaks. They may also be effective for diarrhoea). In fact modern bagpipe-makers recommend rather more effective (and less smelly) materials which work very well. The Music Shop in Lostwithiel supplied mine. In modern western bagpipes the bag is covered with a cloth bag-cover, which can be a Scottish tartan beautifully decorated with fringes and braiding. In the middle ages the bag-cover was probably dyed some bright colour, such as red, blue, or green. As well as its "top coat" the bagpipes can also have underclothes (white of course) to prevent the revolting contents of the bag (e.g. spit and fermenting treacle) from staining the beautiful bag-cover.

In primitive bagpipes the pipes, with their reeds attached, were simply tied into the holes in the bag with string. This is not really a very good idea, because every time the reeds get sodden, or need adjusting, the whole thing has to be untied. Even if you are a Boy Scout, untying the knots is tedious. Also the delicate reeds are just poking inside the bag, and if you are in a plane crash or somebody sits on your bag, the reeds will never be the same again. Modern bagpipes have cylindrical wooden stocks permanently tied into the bag, and the blowpipe, chanters and drones slide into holes bored in the stocks. The stocks are long enough to protect the reeds and enable the pipes to be easily withdrawn for reed adjustments.

The blowpipe is fitted with a non-return valve at the bottom to retain the air between puffs of wind, and prevent the unmentionable contents of the bag from flowing back into the mouth. Most types of bagpipe have short blowpipes, but the Scottish Highland Bagpipe has a long one, which enables the player to hold his head proudly erect and display his magnificent instrument to the full.

The chanter or chanters are fitted to the chanter stock at the front end of the bag, so they can be tilted downwards in front of the player's body and easily manipulated by the fingers.

The drones are fitted to drone stocks along the top of the bag, and normally rest on the player's shoulder. In the Scottish Highland Bagpipe the largest, or bass drone, rests against the player's ear, and the two smaller tenor drones are attached to the bass drone with ornamental cords. On some types of bagpipe, drones can also be fitted to a large chanter stock.

In folk instruments the woodwork is very crude, as indeed it must be if made by a shepherd in the mountains. He has plenty of time, dead sheep and trees but little else. The Scottish Highland Bagpipe at the other extreme can be made a magnificent instrument, with beautifully turned wooden parts of ebony, cocus wood or Brazil wood, embellished with silver and ivory.

PETER O'DOHERTY, THE AUTHOR, AND MERVYN DAVEY AT
LOWENDER PIRAN, WITH THEIR CORNISH BAGPIPES
Photo: Matthew Clarke

Chapter 3

HISTORY (WITH SOME GEOGRAPHY)

Reed-pipes, which are the basis of the bagpipes, are very ancient indeed. You would think the single pipe must have come before the double pipe, but nevertheless double pipes have been found in the Sumarian city of Ur, dating from about 2500 B.C. They are of silver, but very slender, no doubt copying their more humble prototype made of cane. There are carvings of people playing such double pipes in ancient Sumaria. As far as we know, these are the earliest actual specimens of musical pipe yet discovered.

We do not know the name of the piper of Ur, but in Egypt a set of divergent double pipes was found beside their owner in a mummy case. They belonged to The Lady Maket, so the first piper we know by name was a woman. The pipes probably date from about 1200 B.C. Six reed pipes were later found next to the mummy of an unknown woman, also in Egypt. Feminists please note that piping has never been confined to men.

Pictorial representations of double pipes continue down the ages for a thousand years. The Greek writer Strabo (born 64 B.C.) tells us that centuries ago the Phoenicians came to trade in tin to the Cassiterides, which may have been the Isles of Scilly (or St. Michael's Mount, or lots of other places too). The Phoenicians certainly had double divergent pipes, so it is possible our Cornish ancestors heard the sound of the ancestors of the bagpipes several thousand years ago.

It is very difficult to decide when and where the bag was first used. There is the reference by Aristophanes in the fourth century B.C., then in the Berlin Staatliches Museum there is a strange terracotta figure from Alexandria dating from about the last century B.C. As far as we know this is the earliest representation of a bag being used to play a musical pipe. The figure is wearing a splendid conical hat and playing the panpipes with his left hand. With his right hand he is holding a pipe attached to a bag under his left arm. It is far from clear how the bag was inflated.

The first mention of the bag-pipe by name (in Latin: Utricularius) is by the writer Suetonius, concerning the Roman emperor Nero in the first

DETAIL FROM LUTTRELL PSALTER, c. 1330
"The Bagpipe" by Francis Collinson. Routledge & Kegan Paul

"THE BAGPIPER", BY ALBRECHT DÜRER
"The Bagpipe" by Francis Collinson. Routledge & Kegan Paul

century A.D. I learned as a boy that Nero fiddled while Rome burned, but did not realise that when he was not being one of the worst tyrants the world has ever known, he was an accomplished singer and performer on the lyre (no doubt he was an accomplished liar as well).

As every schoolboy knows, the Romans came to Britain in 55 B.C. Even if the bagpipes were not used here already, the Romans must have brought their musical instruments with them during their occupation which lasted until about 400 A.D. Unfortunately there is no positive evidence of this on coins, statues, or literature.

As Britain entered the dark ages, the bagpipe evidence disappears completely, until manuscripts of the thirteenth and fourteenth centuries, which show a bag attached to a single chanter with no drones. The Pipers Stone at Ford Church, Northumberland (thirteenth century) appears to show a bagpipe with one chanter, as does a fourteenth century carving in a church in Hull.

From the fourteenth century we begin to see bagpipes with a single drone as well as a chanter. They can be seen at Honington, Suffolk; Melrose Abbey, Scotland; Finchingfield Church, Essex, and Beverley Minster.

From the sixteenth century we also find carvings of bagpipes with two chanters. As well as the Cornish examples we are saving until later, they can be seen at St. Mary's Church, Warwick; the Priory Church, Great Malvern, Worcestershire; Hexham Abbey, Northumberland; St. Mary's Church, Shrewsbury, and East Harling Church, Norfolk. (Although I spent a morning hunting for the latter without success).

Also in the sixteenth century came pictures on the continent of Europe of bagpipes with two drones. The earliest and best known is "Der Dudelsachpfeifer" (1514) by Dürer, now in Vienna. There are also many woodcuts by Hans Holbein the Younger (1497-1543). No doubt two drones also appeared in Britain at the same time, but British pictures or carvings are rare in this period. William Hogarth (1697-1764) shows bagpipes with two drones in many of his pictures of English life.

The earliest known carving of a bagpipe with three drones is the sculpture "The Bagpipe Boy" by C. G. Cibber (1630-1700). He was "Carver to the King's Closet", which is a rather splendid-sounding title.

William Shakespeare mentions the bagpipe several

"THE BAGPIPE BOY", BY CIBBER (1630-1700). THE FIRST REPRESENTATION KNOWN OF BAGPIPES WITH 3 DRONES
Perran Truran

times. In "The Merchant of Venice" he confuses everybody by calling them "woollen bagpipes". They could I suppose, have been primitive bagpipes with wool on the outside, but it is more likely that he meant "Uilleann" pipes.

Throughout their long history the bagpipes were mainly folk instruments played by shepherds, and by wandering minstrels who would play at weddings and local feasts and celebrations. However, they were also played in high places. The inventory of musical instruments of King Henry VIII includes five sets of bagpipes. One was "A Baggepipe with pipes of ivorie, the bagge covered with purple vellat." Earlier kings of England had "pipes" and "pipers", but whether they had bags or not it is difficult to be sure.

It is clear that bagpipes were once played all over Britain, but by the end of the eighteenth century the English bagpipes were virtually extinct, except in Northumberland, just south of the border.

The Northumberland small-pipe still survives, and has a beautiful soft sound suitable for playing indoors. It has a single chanter usually fitted with keys to make the playing of sharps and flats easier, and four drones, three of which are used at a time. The chanter is fitted with a double reed, and the drones with single reeds. All the bores are cylindrical. The bag is supplied with air not by the mouth, but with bellows held under the right arm. The left arm controls the supply of wind to the pipes by squeezing the bag. The end of the chanter is closed, not open, so when all the fingers are down the sound is stopped, making it possible to play detached notes. The Northumberland small-pipe is really no relation of the Scottish Highland Bagpipe, and was probably developed from the French instrument, the musette.

There were once Scottish small-pipes too, but they have long since been eclipsed by the Scottish Highland Bagpipes, synonymous with the word bagpipe all over the world. They are definitely not quiet instruments, and are heard at their best played out of doors either solo or en masse as in the Edinburgh military tattoo. They have a single conical chanter with a double reed, and three drones with cylindrical bores and single reeds. The Scottish Highland Bagpipe has become so successful that it is now played all over the world by people who love bagpipes, and is actually manufactured in India and Pakistan, and exported back to Britain. I examined a Pakistani set recently which was beautifully made, and priced in accordance with the lower wages of craftsmen in the East.

The Irish also had outdoor bagpipes, similar to the Scottish model but having only two drones. However, Ireland is nowadays famous for its "union pipe", or "Uillean pipe", a beautiful indoor instrument not unlike the Northumbrian small-pipe. The chanter has a double reed, a conical bore, and is fitted with keys. Although open at the end, the end can be closed by a leather pad on the player's knee, and the sound thus stopped when required. There are three drones, with double reeds and cylindrical bores, but in addition several regulators with single reeds and conical bores. These are fitted with keys so the harmony can be varied. The Uillean pipes are bellows blown, with the bellows held under the right elbow. "Uillean" is Irish for "elbow".

Wales is famous not so much for its bagpipes as the pibcorn or horn-pipe, an ancient reed-pipe fitted with cow-horns on the end. This instrument

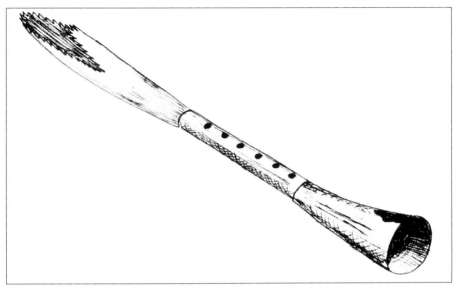

WELSH PIBCORN FROM ANGLESEY

Perran Truran

seems to have been fitted with a bag at some stage in its history. Welsh bagpipes are illustrated in sixteenth-century manuscripts in the British Museum, but sadly they died out long ago.

Turning to Celtic countries overseas, the bagpipes are still very popular in Brittany, and can be heard playing at village festivals, and especially at the marvellous Breton festival at Quimper. As well as the French peasant bagpipe, the Bretons play the biniou, a delightful miniature outdoor instrument. In Galicia, in North West Spain, they play the gaita, with a chanter and one bass drone.

Nearly every country in the world has some bagpipe history, but in the Cornish context the most interesting instrument outside Britain is the zampogna from southern Italy and Sicily. It has a single stock, bored to take two drones and two chanters. The chanters are of unequal length, and played with two hands independently. The chanter for the right hand plays six notes, and that for the left, five notes. It is thus the only surviving bagpipe which can play two independent melodies, as well as drones. The chanters end in large flared bells. The zampogna is also unusual in that it uses double reeds throughout; for the drones as well as the chanters. We will describe the special music it plays in the next chapter.

Of the thousands of bagpipes which must have been made over the ages, only a tiny fraction have survived. Peasant instruments would rapidly become smelly, decompose and fall to pieces. There would be no reason for anyone to try to preserve them - they simply made a new set. Expensive instruments, perhaps with ivory ornamentation, would be much more likely to be preserved, even if the bag had to be renewed. Even so, few of them remain. The present day interest in things which are old is quite a recent phenomenon. Even less bagpipe music survives, so here we are left with a great deal of guesswork.

ITALIAN BAGPIPE
Pitt Rivers Museum, Oxford

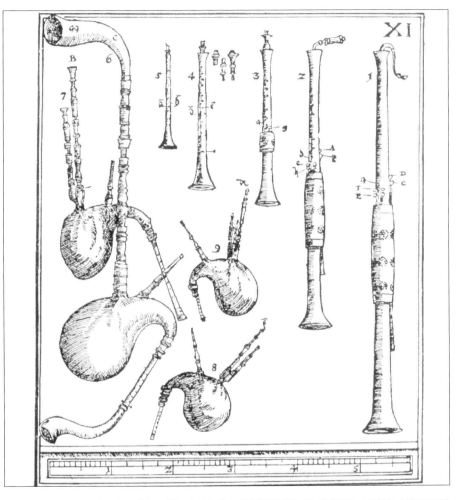

PRAETORIUS DRAWING, 1619. 1 TO 5 ARE SHAWMS, 6 TO 9 ARE BAGPIPES
"Woodwind Instruments & Their History" by Anthony Baines. Faber & Faber

Chapter 4

THE MUSIC

When we think of "music" today, we think of staff notation with its staffs of five lines on which are placed the notes. However, this is a comparatively recent development, dating from about the sixteenth century. In the twelfth century there was a rudimentary notation developed for plain song, but before that tunes were memorised, and passed down from father to son or teacher to pupil, by ear. (As a matter of interest, the Chinese had a musical notation in 1000 B.C.).

The shepherd bagpipe of the dark ages must have played what we now call folk tunes, which would be known and sung by the local village people. Today, classical music and "pop" music are kept quite separate. It would be very odd to hear the BBC Symphony orchestra playing Country and Western Music. Even in Handel's day the distinction was not drawn so sharply: he wrote many splendid dance tunes and popular songs.

Throughout the middle ages the bagpiper must have been very popular, playing at local feasts, dances, and weddings. Until the mid eighteenth century, songs and dances were usually one and the same: nearly all dances also had words. Although no music specifically for the bagpipes has come down to us from this period, hundreds of country dances survive, most of which must have been played on the bagpipes at some time. Some of the tunes seem to imply a drone accompaniment; these were almost certainly intended for the bagpipes.

By the end of the fifteenth century there were town "waits" or minstrels, who were public servants employed by the town. In England there was usually a band, consisting mainly of shawms, of four to six players, but in Scotland there was usually a town piper, perhaps with a drummer. The musicians, their instruments, and their livery were paid for by a levy on householders. The piper at Dalkeith wore a long yellow coat lined with red, red plush breeches, white stockings and shoes with buckles. The Scottish piper's duty was to play through the streets of the town in the morning to wake up its citizens, and again in the evening to serenade them to bed. In

Dundee, Jedburgh and Lanark the piper's round started at 4 a.m., (under penalty of losing his wages and eight days' imprisonment). At Perth and Dalkeith the citizens were lazy, and did not want to be wakened until 5 a.m. I'm afraid this early rising would not be very popular today. The pipers were often provided with a house to live in: the "Piper's House" still survives in Jedburgh.

In England, as well as Scotland, bagpipers were asked to play at the harvesting and sheep-shearing; and at Gateshead in 1633 they were paid 3/4d to play for five days to the road menders. Road making in those days must have been a rather quieter operation than it is today.

There are even records of the bagpipes being played in church, but generally speaking the Church of Scotland was not amused by the bagpipes, and pipers were often fined, jailed, or banished for playing on the Sabbath.

Music has been employed in battle since very early times: the ancient Egyptian soldiers for example were often depicted playing wind instruments. The harp was the traditional instrument of most Celtic countries and, rather surprisingly, it seems to have been played in battle too. It is hard to imagine anything less suitable for exhorting the troops than the feeble twanging of the Celtic harp. It could only have been heard by a tiny group of soldiers within a few yards. It might improve the troops with thoughts of heaven after they had been killed but that seems to me a rather negative approach to a battle! The bagpipes, on the other hand, are just ideal for battle use. Their stirring sounds are just the thing to improve bravery and determination. There is a tradition that the Scottish Highland Bagpipe was first played in 1314, at the battle of Bannockburn, and they were certainly played at the many Scottish battles in the next centuries.

The year 1746 was bad news for Scottish Military pipers. James Reid, one of the pipers in Ogilvie's regiment, was one of the highlanders who garrisoned Carlisle during the 1745 rebellion. When Carlisle was captured by the Hanovarian army he was taken prisoner and tried at York on 2nd October 1746. His plea was that he was not a soldier, but only a piper. Unfortunately the court ruled that the bagpipe was an instrument of war. James was executed in November. A disarming act passed the same year made illegal the wearing of the traditional Highland dress, or the carrying of arms, including by inference the bagpipe. I cannot think of any other example of a musical instrument being made illegal, except perhaps the Street Act which had the effect of driving the barrel pianos off the streets of London.

From about 1600 the Scottish pipers invented their own system of musical notation, called Canntaireachd (Gaelic for "chanting"). It was a sort of tonic sol-fa system, where each syllable indicated the note to be played, and the ornaments or twiddly-bits before and after the note. Here is an example:

Hiodroho Hodroho, Haninen Hiechin,
Hodraha Hodroho, Hodroho Hachin,
Hiodroho Hodroho, Haninen Hiechin,
Hodraha Hodraha, Hodraha Hodraha,
Hodraha Hodraha, Hodraha Hachin.

The highest form of the Scottish bagpipers' art is the Piobaireachd, or Ceol Mor, the "great music" of the pipes. These musical "symphonies" date from about 1600, and were written to celebrate great events, such as battles or the deaths of great warriors. They consisted of a slow melody, followed by sets of elaborate variations, followed by a repeat of the melody itself.

It will be appreciated that on all bagpipes where the end of the chanter cannot be closed (that is, all except the Irish and Northumberland small pipes) it is impossible to stop the note until the bag is deflated at the end of the piece. To give the illusion of articulation, the bagpiper plays very fast notes (called grace notes) either before or after the note itself. The performance of these grace notes is a vital part of the art of bagpiping, and features predominantly in Piobaireachd.

You do not have to be musical to realise that the notes played on a bagpipe chanter do not conform to any known scale. Originally the fingerholes were the same diameter and spaced equally apart, giving a scale which does not correspond to either the white or the black notes on the piano. Although this makes it very difficult to mix the bagpipes with other types of instruments, the strange scale contributes greatly to the haunting sound of bagpipes, and makes them sound quite unlike any other instrument.

For more than twenty years I have played the clarinet in amateur symphony orchestras. One day I went to see my distinguished neighbour: a Scottish doctor who was a piper, and had retired to Cornwall. He dismissed my achievement on the clarinet in a few sentences.

He said that Beethoven wrote his music in a funny scale which cannot be played on the bagpipes.

He said that at the great music festivals one adjudicator could judge the performance of a whole symphony orchestra. On the other hand, it took half a dozen adjudicators just to judge one Scottish bagpiper.

As I learned to my cost, it takes a great deal of blow to play the bagpipes. Although you can release the arm pressure on the bag slightly while you are blowing, this has to be done with very great skill, or the pitch of the notes falls, creating the general effect of a run-down gramophone. If

CHRISTMAS PIPING IN ITALY, 1830

"The Oxford Companion to Music" by Percy A. Scholes, 9th Edition 1955, by permission of Oxford University Press

the bag is old and leaky, the player has to be a superman to keep things going. In Scotland there is a flat stone by the roadside inscribed "Piper's Grave". It is where a piper dropped dead having tried, for a bet, to play his pipes up a long hill on a hot summer's day.

In the 18th century, schools of bagpiping were established in Scotland, which became very famous. They would not have got on very well with the modern educational experts and their "instant learning". The old Scottish pupils used to study for seven years, and since the bagpipe is only capable of playing eight notes, that averages out at 1.143 notes per year. At that rate it would take 100 years to learn the piano!

There is a very ancient tradition that the sound of the pipes is a good cure for rheumatism. Certainly I have never felt better than after hearing the pipes outside Edinburgh Castle. On the other hand hearing myself play inside a small room has great therapeutic effects too - I feel so much better when I stop.

We will end this chapter with a look at the music of the Italian zampogna: the bagpipe with the two chanters. These chanters of unequal length could play two tunes at once, or, more usually, play a series of chords to support the playing of a shrill type of shawm called the piffaro, by a second player. The players are traditionally shepherds, who come down into the towns during the Novena days before Christmas, and play Christmas music in front of shrines, and along the streets. Many years ago the more adventurous of these players used to travel all over Europe, making the zampogna the best known form of bagpipe before the Scottish Highland Bagpipe attained its present position of pre-eminence. The traditional Christmas music they played had a strong influence on eighteenth century composers, and Handel, for example, imitated their music in the famous "Pastoral Symphony" from the "Messiah". The original score is marked "Piva", an Italian word for bagpipe.

PASTORAL SYMPHONY FROM THE MESSIAH, BY G. F. HANDEL

Chapter 5

THE CORNISH BAGPIPES

Since it would be a miracle if an actual set of Cornish bagpipes came to light, we have to make do with what survives in literature, folk-lore and in carvings.

The story of the Cornish language is as fascinating as that of the bagpipes, and of course its roots are just as ancient. The Celts came to Britain from Central Europe about 600 B.C., and when the Romans came in 55 B.C. they found the islands inhabited by Celtic tribes. The Roman historians described these Britons, with their priestly druids and their impressive stone monuments. The Celtic religion taught the doctrine of everlasting life, and the druids were widely respected throughout Europe.

The Romans left Britain in the fifth century A.D., and shortly afterwards, Britain was invaded by the warlike pagan Saxons. Thousands of Celts fled from the onslaught, many of them to what is now Brittany ("little Britain"). They also fled to Galicia in north-west Spain - another stronghold of the bagpipe. In time the Celts were forced into the extremities of Britain: Cornwall, Wales, the Isle of Man, and Scotland and Ireland where they mingled with the Celts already there. The Scottish, Manx and Irish Celts spoke what is now known as Goidelic Celtic, and the Cornish, Welsh and Breton Celts spoke Brythonic or "British", Celtic.

Very little survives of the original Celtic language of mainland Europe, and as the Celtic peoples were divided, so their languages drifted apart, until today there are six separate but related Celtic languages: Cornish, Welsh, Breton, Irish, Scottish Gaelic, and Manx. Sadly, the Cornish language ceased to be generally spoken in the eighteenth century, and the Manx language in this century. The other four languages survive, but survival is a struggle.

Irish has a rich literature going back to the seventh century, and Welsh is almost as rich, with documents surviving from the twelfth century. Possession of a literature is a great incentive to learn a language. If the language is no longer spoken, and there is little to read, only the most determined scholars are likely to bother to learn it.

Sadly, very little Cornish literature survives, all of it in manuscript, and nothing in print. For centuries Cornish was the language of the common people: farmers, fishermen, and miners; very few of whom could read or write. Those that had the time, money, and inclination, spent their limited resources on learning a more useful language - English. From the tenth century we have some "glosses", or notes in the margin, written in Cornish to explain a Latin text. From the twelfth century we have the "vocabularium cornicum", a seven page manuscript giving the meaning of 961 Cornish words in Latin. These fragments are virtually all that is left of "Old Cornish", but by good luck there are 15 words of great musical interest. Unfortunately there was no common Latin word for "bagpipe", so we obviously cannot expect to find its exact Cornish equivalent in a Latin-Cornish list. However, the following entries appear:

FELLORES	a female fiddler
HARFEL	a viol, fiddle
HARFELLOR	a fiddler
KENIAT	a singer, player
KENIAT/COBRICA	a horn-pipe player
PIB	a musical pipe
PIPHIT	a piper
PIBONOUL	a pipe, flute

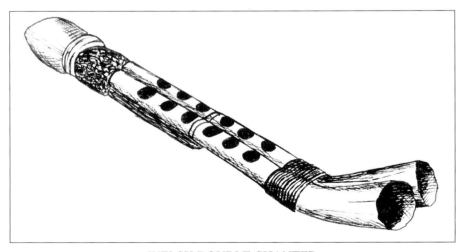

WELSH DOUBLE CHANTER

Perran Truran

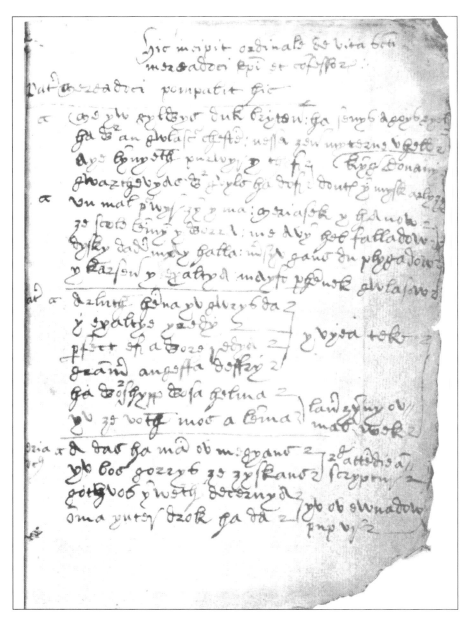

A PAGE FROM BEUNANS MERIASEK, THE LIFE OF ST. MERIASEK, 1504
"The Cornish Language & its Literature" by P. Beresford Ellis. Routledge & Kegan Paul

The horn-pipe is a rustic instrument, long obsolete, closely related to the bagpipe but having no bag. It has one or two chanters, terminated at the bottom by a cow horn. The "pipe" very likely meant the bagpipe, but it could have meant a primitive flute or shawm, the ancestor of the modern oboe. These Cornish words from the very remote past at least tell us that there were active musicians in Cornwall.

In Medieval times the Cornish spoke what is now known as Middle Cornish. Several Cornish gentlemen used Cornish in their coats of arms, and the collegiate church of St. Thomas of Canterbury at Glasney, Penryn, became the centre of written Cornish. A manuscript from there dated 1265 contains the first complete sentence in Cornish which has come down to us. Unfortunately it does not mention the bagpipes.

Glasney was the place where the three Cornish miracle plays, or Ordinalia, were probably written in the fourteenth century. These were "The Beginning of the World", "The Passion of Christ", and "The Resurrection of Our Lord". The earliest copy of the Ordinalia, dating from the fifteenth century, is now in the Bodleian Library, Oxford, but it was transcribed and translated in 1859, and parts of it are also available in modern editions. There was also another miracle play, Beunans Meriasek, the life of St.

ST. JUST PLEN-AN-GWARY
"The Life of the Cornish" by Crysten Fudge. Truran Publications

Meriasek, Bishop of Vannes in Brittany. The earliest copy of this is dated 1504.

Miracle plays were not confined to Cornwall, but were performed all over Europe. They still survive in the Passion Play performed every ten years at Oberammergau in South Germany. Although there is nothing very special about the *content* of the Cornish miracle plays, they are by far the most important source of knowledge we have of the Cornish *language*. Miracle plays, and no doubt other less dignified events, took place all over Cornwall in a village open air theatre, or Plen An Gwary. Few survive today, although there is still an excellent example right in the centre of St. Just in Penwith, near Lands End. A book by Jenner contains a list of over 80 sites which existed in former times.

The miracle plays contain four references to pipes. Although again the word for pipe does not mean specifically bagpipes, it is very likely that this is what was intended. The references are:

Origo Mundi (The Beginning of The World)
> The last stanza:
> A barth a'n tas menstrels a ras
> Pebough whare
> In the name of the Father; minstrels, I pray
> Pipe immediately.

Resurrexio Domini (The Resurrection of Our Lord)
> The last stanza:
> Emperor:
> Now menstrels pybych bysy
> May hyllyn mos the thonssye
> Now minstrels, pipe diligently,
> That we may go to dance.

Beunans Meryasek (The Life of Meriasek)
> Lines 2511-2512:
> Pybugh menstrels colonnek
> May hyllyn donsia dyson
> Pipe you, hearty minstrels,
> That we may dance without delay.
> Lines 4563-4565:
> Pyboryon wethugh in scon
> Ny a vyn ketep map bron
> Moys the donsya

DOLLY PENTREATH, PORTRAIT BY JOHN OPIE AT ST. MICHAEL'S MOUNT
"The Death of Cornish" by P. A. S. Pool
Portrait reproduced by kind permission of Lord St Levan

DOLLY PENTREATH'S MEMORIAL, PAUL CHURCH

"The Cornish Language and its Literature" by Beresford Ellis, Routledge & Kegan Paul

Pipers, blow quickly,
We will, every son of a breast,
Go to dance.

A passion poem entitled Pascon Agan Arluth also survives. The earliest version was found in Sancreed church, and dates from the fifteenth century (no bagpipes!)

In 1611 William Jordan wrote another miracle play called "The Creation of the World", although it is likely that he merely copied it from an earlier source. There is a reference to pipes in this too:

Gwreans An Bys (The Creation of the World)

Last stanza:
Mynstrels growgh theny peba
May hallan warbarthe downssy
Del ew an vaner han geys
Minstrels, do ye pipe to us,
That we may together dance,
As is the manner and the jest (custom)

("Heare endeth the creacon of the worlde wth noyes flude wryten by William Jordan : the XIIth of August 1611").

These important references show that there was a tradition of piping and dancing in Cornwall in the middle ages, and possibly as late as 1611.

Several Cornish vocabularies were produced in the eighteenth century: by Edward Lluyd in 1707, "Antiquities of Cornwall" by Dr. W. Borlase in 1754 and 1769, and "Archaeologia Cornu-Britannia" by William Pryce in 1790. These repeat many of the words in the Vocabularium Cornicum, but some of them seem to have acquired extra meanings, for example in Archaeologia Cornu-Britannia "Fellores a female fiddler" has become "Fellores a player on the pipe, or violin; a woman piper". "Harfel a viol, fiddle" has become "Harfel a she piper; a viol, a harp". "Harfellor a fiddler" has become "Harfellor a player on the pipe". After a gap of six centuries the words seem to have been expanded to include wind instruments as well as strings.

In the Borough Accounts for St. Ives 1570-1639, there are several references to a town drummer, and one item about the year 1575 for "Itm Payd to the Pypers for there wages". (Town clerk's spelling not mine!)

Camborne Churchwarden's accounts for 1550 contain the item: "Paid to the Piper in the Play 4d".

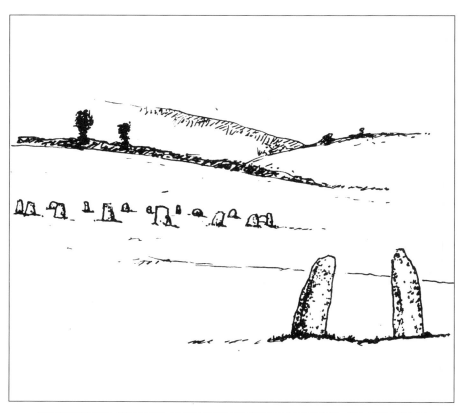

THE PIPERS STONES AND THE MERRY MAIDENS, ST. BURYAN

Keith Spurgin

When we turn to Cornish folk-lore we are on shakier, but more entertaining ground. Most visitors to Cornwall have heard of the "Merry Maidens" stone circle, with the two "Pipers" menhirs standing close by. They are to be found on the south coast road from Lamorna to Land's End: the Merry Maidens on one side of the road and the "Pipers" on the other. Learned historians have studied their function and origin, but the bagpipes do not appear in their conclusions. However, Robert Hunt, a collector of folk-lore during the 19th century, gives the following account:

"In the Parish of Burian are the Dawns Myin or Men - the dancing stones - commonly called the Merry Maidens; and near them are two granite pillars, named the Pipers. One sabbath evening some of the thoughtless maidens of the neighbouring village, instead of attending vespers, strayed into the fields, and two evil spirits, assuming the guise of pipers, began to play some dance tunes. The young people yielded to the temptation; and forgetting the holy day, commenced dancing. The excitement increased with the exercise, and soon the music and the dance became extremely wild; when lo a flash of lightning from the clear sky transfixed them all, the tempters and the tempted, and there in stone they stand."

There are similar stories relating to the "Hurlers" stone circles on Bodmin Moor, and the "Nine Maidens" stone row near St. Columb Major, but such stories are not confined to Cornwall, and occur all over Europe. It would be great fun to photograph the pipers stones using intense side illumination, or infra-red light, to discover the actual shape and form of the Cornish bagpipes, but I think a very powerful computer and lots of Cornish cyder would be needed to interpret the results.

The stone carver and the wood carver have left us the most important clues about the Cornish Bagpipes. There are stone carvings on St. Austell parish church tower; Launceston's church of St. Mary and a stone on private land on Bodmin Moor, and wood carvings on bench ends in the churches in Altarnun† and Davidstow. Of these only three still reveal any detail, but the fascinating thing is that all three show a bagpipe with one trumpet-like drone and two chanters.

The carving on St. Austell church tower is the top right-hand gargoyle on the west side above the west door. It can easily be seen by standing on the market steps and craning your neck. Everybody will either think you are mad, or think you are me. It is very difficult to photograph because of the combination of bad accessibility and poor light, but some excellent photographs were taken from the right side only when the tower was in scaffolding a few years ago. The surviving detail is fantastic:

The player is a grotesque man with huge eyes and his hair standing on end. Perhaps he is afraid of heights. He is holding the bag under his right arm, like the piper's carvings at Altarnun and Davidstow, but unlike the modern Scottish piper, who always uses his left. Early pictures of bagpipers usually show the bag under the left arm, but notable exceptions are the 1514 painting by Dürer already mentioned; a plate in a book "Theophilia" by Benlowes (1652); a picture "The Dance of Death" (16th century), and numerous pictures by Hogarth (18th century). This is probably not an

† With apologies to the locals who would spell it Altarnon. The patron saint is St. Nonna.

"THE DANCE OF DEATH", 16TH CENTURY
"Bagpipes in English Works of Art", by Dr R. D. Cannon
Galpin Society Journal, Volume XLII

important point anyway. Many bagpipes are so flexible that they can be played either way - the player can please himself according to whether he is right or left handed, or whether he reckons one arm is stronger. Sculptors and artists may not have noticed which side the bag was in any case and just put it where it looked nice. It is most unlikely that a sculptor or artist would ever employ a model to sit with his bagpipes while he was consigned to immortality. However, the St. Austell bagpipes are definitely not flexible. The mouthpipe, drone and chanters seem to be fixed to a common rigid stock, so that the drone has to rest on the left shoulder, and thus the bag has to go under the right arm.

GARGOYLE ON ST. AUSTELL
CHURCH TOWER, TAKEN FROM
SCAFFOLDING DURING REPAIR
WORK
Photo: Carl Roberts

GARGOYLE ON ST. AUSTELL
CHURCH TOWER, TAKEN FROM
SCAFFOLDING DURING REPAIR
WORK
Photo: Drewitt & Drewitt, Penzance

GARGOYLE ON ST. AUSTELL CHURCH TOWER, TAKEN FROM BELOW
WITH TELEPHOTO LENS

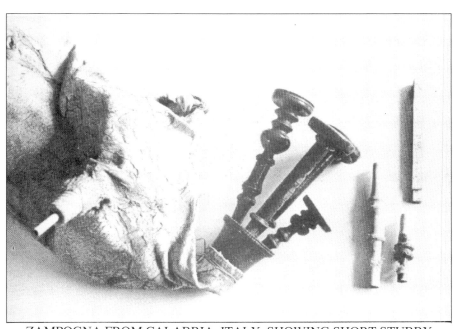

ZAMPOGNA FROM CALABRIA, ITALY, SHOWING SHORT STUBBY
CHANTERS, LIKE THOSE ON ST. AUSTELL CHURCH
" An unusual Italian Bagpipe" , by S. Jensen and T. R. Anderson, Galpin Society Journal,
Volume XXIX

The drone portrayed must have been turned on a lathe, because it is a most ornate affair, with a large flared trumpet-like bell, and several ornamental collars. One has a pattern of holes all round it. The central collar is almost certainly meant to be the tuning slide. There is so much detail that it would be possible to make a perfect replica of the outside. The inside remains a mystery, but the outside shape looks as if it has a cylindrical bore, with a conical flare at the end.

The two chanters are played with a hand each, and are splayed out at an angle of about 18 degrees. It is even possible to see the fingerholes. The left chanter has two open holes at the top, which doesn't seem very likely, and two open holes at the bottom which could easily be tuning holes. The right chanter has one open hole at the top and one at the bottom. The chanters are too chubby to be realistic, but look definitely conical, so presumably the bores were conical too. The sculptor has even hollowed out the inside of the bells to make them look more natural. The two chanters are fitted into a large stock, which seems to be carved with a spiral at the top and a bunch of grapes below. The player's right hand is slightly higher than his left (like Davidstow, but unlike Altarnun).

The carving is in Pentewan stone, like the rest of the tower. This rock has the same composition as a biotite granite, but occurs in thin bands on "dykes" around the outside of the main mass of granite. The latter cooled from its molten state slowly, giving rise to large crystals, while the dykes cooled quickly, giving a fine grained acid igneous rock which is easier to carve than granite, and takes fine detail well. The stone for the tower actually came from small quarries near the cliffs at Pentewan. A light-coloured band of rock can easily be seen from a boat offshore.

The chanters may have been made chubby because of the rather brittle Pentewan stone, but very similar chanters have been found in Calabria, in Southern Italy, and were described in the Galpin Society Journal for May 1976.

There was a church in St. Austell on the present site in the twelfth century. A document dated 1169 mentions the "Sanctuarium De Sancto Austolon", but most of the present building dates from the 15th century. The tower was probably finished between 1478 and 1485, and is 94 feet high. All the stone sculptures on the west side of the tower are remarkably fine, and are described and highly praised by A. L. Rowse in his book "St. Austell". The tower is what is known as the "Somerset type", and towers of a similar style stretch right across the west country. A great deal of church building was going on in the fifteenth century, and the work was done by teams of travelling craftsmen based in Devon or Somerset. Many of these were foreign workers.

We are left with more mysteries. The Cornish bagpipe carving could have been:

1. Carved by a Cornishman to represent the Cornish bagpipes he knew. He might even have been a piper himself.
2. Carved by a member of the Somerset/Devon team to represent bagpipes he had seen in Cornwall.
3. Carved by somebody who had seen an Italian zampogna player, somewhere in Britain, probably at Christmas time.
4. Carved by somebody who was given a sketch of a bagpipe to copy - which could have come from anywhere.
5. Carved by an Italian craftsman, who would naturally portray the zampogna he knew.

What do you think?

The church of St. Mary Magdalene in Launceston was started in 1511 and completed and consecrated in 1524, but minor additions were made until 1538. The church is built of granite, and the east outside wall is lavishly decorated with carvings of musicians, including a bagpiper. Unfortunately, although granite is more durable than Pentewan stone, the coarse crystals of felspar, quartz and mica tend to break off under the sculptor's chisel, so intricate detail is never attempted. We are therefore left with what is clearly a piper, but with no details. The minstrels portrayed on the church are well documented in the borough accounts. For example an entry for 1467 reads "One quart of wine expended by the Mayor and his companions and the Mynstrelles in the vigil of the Blessed Mary Magdalene". It sounds as if they had a jolly good time. I bet the bagpiper drank more than his share. The minstrels gained notoriety in 1440 when Bishop Lacy granted a forty days' indulgence to all true penitents who gave money to support them. An indulgence simply meant that all your sins were forgiven for the period specified. What a marvellous recipe for unlimited debauchery. The bishop is said to have granted this indulgence because of an incident which occurred during his visit to Launceston on 15th June 1440. He had come from Okehampton and was no doubt tired and weary after bumping along the rough roads in his carriage. As he came up the hill to Launceston he heard the strains of the Minstrels welcoming him from the hill-top, and is said to have exclaimed "Holy Mother of Jesus, 'tis the angels

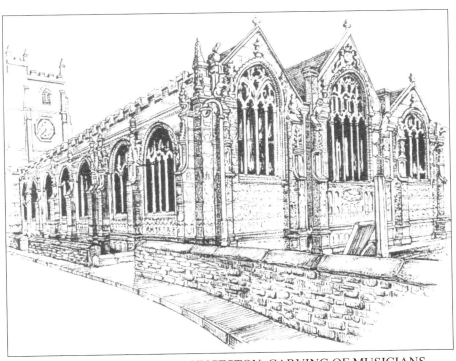

ST. MARY'S CHURCH, LAUNCESTON, CARVING OF MUSICIANS
"Cornish Churches" by Joan Rendell, Bossiney Books

CLOSE-UP OF BAGPIPER ON LAUNCESTON CHURCH
Photo: John Black

OLD PHOTOGRAPH OF GRANITE CARVING ON A FARM ON BODMIN MOOR

PILE OF ROCKS OUTSIDE A FARM ON BODMIN MOOR, "ANGEL WITH BAGPIPES" IN CENTRE BELOW CROSS

CLOSE UP OF TOP OF "ANGEL WITH BAGPIPES", BODMIN MOOR

singing", and named the place Angel Hill.

On the edge of Bodmin Moor is an absolutely gorgeous ancient farm, and in the garden is a carved granite figure of an "angel with bagpipes". It would not be fair to tell you exactly where it is. The farmer and his wife were most kind and hospitable to me, but too much interest in the carving could of course become a nuisance. A previous owner of the farm seems to have collected bits and pieces of stonework from round about, and piled them into a heap in the corner of his garden. On the top is a magnificent granite circle with a cross carved on it. Amongst the bits and pieces underneath is a piece of granite about two feet high, now overgrown with ivy and with the bottom parts buried. My wife and I spent hours trying to photograph it, using the farmer's mirror to reflect the sunlight at a glancing angle, but even our best attempt could just as well have been a carving of a helicopter in flight. However, there hangs in a nearby church a photograph taken earlier this century, showing all the stone, including its bottom parts. Furthermore the stone seems to have been in a much better state then. The typed caption reads "Figure of angel with Bagpipes", so somebody either recognised what it was, or had a more vivid imagination than I have.

There is a circular section or "head" at the top, with what looks like a bird in flight carved across it, but I suppose it just could be an angel's face. On its left is an "arm" with a hole in the bottom and an egg inside. It is very hard to imagine it as any possible part of the anatomy of an angel or a bagpipe. On its right is what could be a bag with a mouthpiece coming down from the "head". There is a sort of wheel pattern at the bottom. I have tried holding the photograph upside down and sideways, but it looks less and less like a bagpiper the more I look at it. You try it. A small prize is offered to anyone who can see two chanters while still sober. If, as seems likely, the carving was pinched from the local church, it would date from the fifteenth century, but round about were ancient chapels dating from the twelfth century, long since disappeared.

In Altarnun Church there is an oak bench end depicting a magnificent bagpiper. The piper has a splendid hat slightly reminiscent of Sherlock Holmes, curly hair, and a tunic with a flared skirt. With a lot of imagination it could be a Cornish kilt. He is wearing shoes, and at his feet is a dog. The bag is under his right arm and the mouthpiece and the two chanters are fixed to separate stocks. The chanters are quite unlike the carving on St. Austell church - they are long and slender. The player has a hand for each, and his left hand is lower than his right, and plays on a longer chanter. Fingerholes are visible, but it is impossible to deduce anything meaningful from their positions. The chanters are clearly cylindrical, not conical, although they do have flared bells at the end. There is something very odd about the single drone. It sticks up behind the player's right shoulder at a most unnatural angle, and seems to be fixed to the bag near the bottom end - a most unlikely position. Francis Collinson in his book "The Bagpipe", shows a sketch which leaves the drone out altogether, which I think is going a bit too far. If it were supposed to be a fence post or something, it would have a base near the dog, not be floating in mid-air. I think we must accept that the wood-carver was extremely accurate and realistic, but when he got to the drone, wasn't quite sure what to do with it. Another problem with the drone is that it seems to be

CARVING ON BENCH-END, ALTARNUN CHURCH

Photo: John Black

cylindrical, but its diameter is surely too big in relation to the slender chanters. It has a sort of apology for a bell at the top.

By good fortune we actually know the name of the wood-carver. It is almost unheard of for a church carver to leave his name on his work, but on another pew-end, this one has carved an angel figure with a hat and curly hair, holding a shield which says;

"Robart : Daye

Maker : of this
Worke, & Willyam
Bokimham Curat
John : Hodge Cu
? MD".

The pews were erected when Bishop Oldham was Bishop of Exeter (1507-1523). If you think the spelling is not quite all it might be, please remember that the first English dictionary was not produced by Nathaniel Bailey until 1721. Even Shakespeare did not possess a dictionary.

CARVING ON BENCH-END,
DAVIDSTOW CHURCH
Photo: John Black

At Davidstow, six miles across the moor, there is another oak bench-end depicting a bagpiper: equally magnificent, but quite different. The player looks more like a girl or a young boy than a man, and the carving stops at the bottom of the flared skirt: there are no legs or feet. The player has curly hair sticking out over each ear, and a most curious hat, which could almost be an angel's halo. The bag is under his right arm, but nearly in the front, rather than under the armpit as at Altarnun. Again there are two chanters, one played by each hand, with the right hand lower than the left, but the two chanters are the same length, and conical and chubby compared to the long slender cylindrical chanters at Altarnun. Some finger holes can be seen, but they don't provide any clues as to how the chanters were fingered. The two chanters are fitted to a stock with a rope design carved round it, and the mouthpipe is fitted to a separate stock just behind it, just like the modern Scottish bagpipes. The single drone is a huge conical affair, terminating in a splendid flared bell - rather like the gramophone advertisement for "His Master's Voice". It rests on the player's right shoulder in a reasonably credible way. Unfortunately we do not know the name of the woodcarver, but the bench-ends are thought to date from the sixteenth century.

There was very nearly another bagpipe woodcarving. I had spent the first part of my career in scientific research, and was pretty confident that I knew how to go about it. For months after I retired I searched through the literature at the Institute for Cornish Studies in Redruth, for references to early church music in Cornwall. Eventually I came to their dozens of cardboard box files containing pamphlets on every church in Cornwall, collected by A. K. Hamilton-Jenkin. For many churches there were several pamphlets, but all had to be read, because sometimes their authors were interested in music, and sometimes they weren't. When I reached "St. Neot" there were lots of pamphlets, all extolling the outstanding stained glass windows, but to my delight, one pamphlet described a carving of an angel playing the bagpipes. It did not say exactly where it was, or even if it was a carving in wood or stone, but undoubtedly it was there. I 'phoned the vicar and obtained permission to go and take photographs, but he was very surprised that there was a carving in his church which he had never noticed. I tied a pair of long stepladders to my car roof rack in case the angel was flying high, and set off for St. Neot. With my wife I spent an hour hunting for the bagpipes. There was no problem finding angels - there were angels everywhere. We asked some local people, they had never heard of an angel playing the bagpipes. Finally in exasperation we checked on the pamphlet who was vicar when the bagpiping angel was found. He was not on the list of vicars at St. Neot. Then we checked the saint to whom the church was dedicated. That was different too. Some idiot had put a pamphlet on St. Neot's Church Huntingdon, in the file for St. Neot Cornwall. I felt an idiot too.

What music did these bagpipers play? We can only surmise that they played popular songs and dances of their time. They would have been especially popular for plays, weddings, maypole dancing, and other festivities. They probably also played in the streets and perhaps in the local inns. Bagpipes in churches must surely have been confined to silent carvings!

At one time every town and village in Cornwall had its "feast-day". When I was at Carclaze infant and junior schools we all had a holiday for Carclaze feast day. There were games and dancing, and we were all given lemonade and a saffron bun. In Collectanea Cornubiensia by Boase (1890) there is a list of Cornish feast days which could still be remembered in those days.

A GREEK BAGPIPER FROM THRACE DEMONSTRATING THE DIFFERENT POSITIONS OF THE DRONE. COULD THIS HELP TO EXPLAIN THE PECULIAR DRONE AT ALTARNUN?

"Greek Popular Musical Instruments"
National Bank of Greece

MERVYN DAVEY, HONORARY PIPER TO THE CORNISH GORSEDD, 1986
"Festivals of Cornwall" by Douglas Williams. Bossiney Books

Chapter 6

RECONSTRUCTION

In 1977 Tony Snell explored the possibilities of reconstructing the Cornish bagpipes. David Townsend was involved in the research.

In 1978 Clive Palmer made a set of double chanter, cylindrical-bore pipes based on the bench-end carving at Davidstow.

In 1982 The Celtic Pipe Band, under Pipe Major Bill McColl, arranged Cornish music for the highland pipes. The older Cornish dances and marches were found to adapt particularly well.

In 1983 the Cornish Gorsedd created the office of "Pybyor", or honorary piper, and my good friend Mervyn Davey had the honour of being elected to the post. There being no Cornish bagpipes available at that time, he played his highland pipes, but these are used most effectively in Brittany and in Ireland too.

In 1986 William Coleman adapted traditional Cornish tunes for the "gaita" bagpipe from Galicia in Spain.

In 1988 "PYBA", the Cornish Bagpipes Project, was launched. An excellent booklet, or "Information Pack" was produced which is still available. Revenues from sales of the booklet are used to finance research and development of the Cornish bagpipes. The aims of "PYBA" are:

"Phase I. To recreate the Cornish Bagpipes as a modern working instrument.

"Phase II. To popularise the instrument and its music.

To create a common repertoire of material.

To achieve mastery and excellence in the idiom".

Mervyn Davey has recently taken delivery of a set of Cornish bagpipes, made by a professional to the specification of "PYBA". It looks authentic, and it makes a beautiful Cornish out-door sound. This maker (Chris Bailey) has now made three sets of Cornish pipes based on the Altarnun carving, with a fourth on the way. We shall all be hearing a lot more about these pipes in the future.

As a result of the initial interest created by the PYBA project, a number of other bagpipers in Cornwall have become interested in trying out traditional Cornish music on various types of bagpipes. In the spring of 1993 PYBA entered a new phase by organising concerts using the Cornish

Directors   Will Coleman   0726 815411
Matthew Spring   01 671 9552
Merv Davey   0208 831642

pyba

The Cornish Bagpipe Project

pipes in conjunction with other instruments that are identified with them. Perhaps the most poignant of these was a candle-lit concert in Altarnun Church featuring the Cornish pipes modelled on one bench-end, accompanied by the Cornish Crowd modelled on another. A cassette "Ylow Hengof ha Coth a Gernow" (The Ancient and Traditional Music of Cornwall) has been produced in conjunction with these concerts, and is available from Mervyn Davey.

Mervyn and his colleagues assumed that all original music would have been lost, and that they would have to greatly modify existing Cornish tunes, or write new material in order to establish a repertoire. In fact, this is not proving to be the case. Some of the folk harmonies collected by people like Dr Ralph Dunstan in the 1920s use two parts of very limited range which fit on the pipes with a minimum of adjustment. The "Dilly Carol" even had a drone part in G!

Although it works well as a solo instrument, Mervyn feels that the use of a bombarde/shawm adds much to the sound and seems likely to have been the way it would have been played originally (like the Breton "bombarde and binou" combination).

I am a scientist really, and only an amateur musician, but I have been studying early musical instruments for many years, and making them too. What could I do which would not duplicate the excellent work already done by "PYBA"?

It seemed to me that a resurrected Cornish bagpipe ought to have the following characteristics:

1. It should be mouth-blown.
2. It should have a single bass drone with a single reed and a flared bell.
3. It should have two chanters capable of being played with one hand on each like the Italian zampogna. Despite the slender cylindrical chanters at Altarnun, the resurrected bagpipe should have conical chanters like those at St. Austell and Davidstow, and use double reeds, to give the instrument sufficient power to be played out of doors effectively.

To start off with, and for a bit of fun, I thought I would make an exact copy of one of the chanters on St. Austell Church, using a piece of softwood. The results were awful! I bored a stepped hole through the middle, then reamed it out with a home-made taper reamer, and bored the fingerholes with about the same spacing as in a modern Highland bagpipe. The first problem was that the outside of the chanter was far too fat. Opening the top (thumb) hole actually made the note lower instead of higher, and sometimes, even played a chord which of course is impossible according to the textbooks. The next problem was trying to find a suitable reed to play the brute. None of my reeds would produce a sensible scale, and minute adjustments to the reed produced huge changes in the scale.

Writing this first effort off to experience, I then produced a hardwood chanter with a conical bore and a conical outside too - more like the proportions of the chanters at Altarnun. After hours of tuning and adjustment I finally got it to play, but my best reed had a staple too big to go into the thin end of the bore, so I reamed out the bore to fit the reed, and it played chords again. I was the only bagpipe maker who could play two notes simultaneously on one chanter. Then there was another, insuperable, problem. I have had problems with my chest recently, and the conical bore chanter took more blow than I could muster. Even the thought of playing two of them at once plus a drone made me feel quite ill. Proper bagpipe players are made of sterner stuff. Admitting defeat, I turned two chanters with narrow cylindrical bores, just like Scottish practice chanters in fact. I thought this would be easy, but you try boring 4mm holes, 11 inches long in pieces of seasoned plum. They started off 4mm alright, but by the time I had finished they were 5 or 6mm, and to my amazement, they would not play properly. They had to be exactly 4mm to produce the sound I wanted. The plum wood, by the way, was from an orchard in Golant, on the river Fowey. I had advertised in the local paper twenty years ago for old fruit trees, cut a plum tree down, reduced it to planks, and it had been seasoning ever since. The Lord gave us all patience, and it is free. The real fun started when I tried to tune the fingerholes. Of course the two chanters had to be exactly in tune with each other, and the notes they played varied wildly depending how hard I blew. I made some holes in an old car inner tube, and fitted the double chanter stock, mouthpipe, and a water manometer (a sort of crude pressure gauge). By blowing up the tube to constant pressure I was able eventually to get the two chanters in tune with one another. My neighbours saw me sitting in my conservatory blowing into an inner tube, and heard horrible noises wafting across the garden. All bagpipe makers should live in detached houses in the country, preferably soundproof. It helps if the neighbours are deaf.

Never mind, I thought, making the drone will be easy. It wasn't. I had to make the bore very narrow so it didn't drown the chanters, and it was very difficult to make it sound properly in tune. I used a brass tube between the plumwood parts to make tuning easy and the sudden expansion of the bore caused the notes to break up. Weeks later the whole fantastic contraption was playing in its shiny black inner tube. Now to make it look pretty! With lots of helpful advice from Michael Ransley, my friend the musical instrument maker in Lostwithiel, I bought a piece of suitable leather from Croggon's of Grampound, who have been Cornish tanners for centuries. They supplied the hides to make the Brendan ship for Tim Severin, and were not a bit surprised to be asked for a skin to make a Cornish bagpipe. I cut it out from my template, but could not cope with sewing four layers of leather to make the turn-over seam. The cobbler in Lostwithiel came to my rescue, and did a beautiful job. Within a few hours the inner tube had been thrown away, and a smart leather bag fitted in its place. My wife made a white cover out of an old sheet, to fit over the bag. I did not realise that bagpipes wore underclothes, but of course something has to be done to absorb the treacly glue which is used to seal the leather, and prevent it from spoiling the bag cover itself. This posed a bit of a problem. Nobody has any idea what would have been authentic in the sixteenth century. Possibly a plain coloured cloth, or else just the leather bag with no cover at all. Just for fun I thought I would use a Cornish tartan - black, white, gold, red and blue. The black and white is supposed to represent the Cornish flag of St. Piran, the gold the gorse; the red the beak of the Cornish Chough, and the blue the sea. Of course I knew the pattern was only invented in recent times, but with my tongue in my cheek I wrote to the weaver, and asked for the history and origins of the tartan. I enclosed a stamped addressed envelope, but I'm afraid I never got a reply. A friendly tailor in Falmouth sold me a square of tartan, and my wife made a beautiful outer cover, complete with fringes round the seams.

So now I am the proud owner of a genuine Cornish bagpipe - perhaps only the second to have been made for two hundred years. It is not a real outdoor bagpipe but a gentler sort of instrument suitable for playing indoors when my wife is out.

If I practise hard for twenty years I should be as good as Mervyn Davey!

Perhaps when Cornish people go to heaven, they will be greeted by their angels playing the bagpipes. Then we shall really know what they sound like!

SOPRANO RECORDERS AND BAGPIPES, 1644

"Musical Instruments through the Ages" by Dr Buchner. Spring Books

SHEPHERD BAGPIPER, FROM A JERUSALEM ICON
"Greek Popular Musical Instruments", National Bank of Greece

ACKNOWLEDGEMENTS AND BIBLIOGRAPHY

This book could not have been written without the help and encouragement of Mervyn Davey, honorary piper to the Cornish Gorsedd and Michael Ransley, musical instrument maker in Lostwithiel. Thanks are also due to the authors of many books, all better scholars than I, particularly to Anthony Baines and Francis Collinson.

There are dozens of books about the bagpipes; the Cornish language; Cornish folk-lore, and Cornish churches. Especially recommended are:

'PYBA" The Cornish Bagpipe Project Information Pack,
> obtainable from Mervyn Davey, "MENEGHYJY", Withiel, Bodmin.

'BAGPIPES" by Anthony Baines, Pitt Rivers Museum, Oxford 1960.

'WOODWIND INSTRUMENTS AND THEIR HISTORY"
> by Anthony Baines, Faber and Faber 1962.

'THE BAGPIPE" The History of a Musical Instrument
> by Francis Collinson, Routledge and Kegan Paul 1975.

THE CORNISH LANGUAGE AND ITS LITERATURE"
> by Beresford Ellis, Routledge and Kegan Paul 1974.

Cover photo by courtesy John Redman, Great Fursnewth, Liskeard